Nick's snowman

Story by Annette Smith
Illustrations by Meredith Thomas

"Sally!" shouted Nick.

"Look at the snow!"

Nick and Sally
went downstairs.
They went to see the snow.

"Look at this big snowball," said Nick.

"My little snowball can go up here," said Sally.

"A snowman!" said Nick.
"This is a snowman!"

"Here are the sticks
for the snowman," said Nick.
"Oh, no!
Here come the dogs."

Sally said to the dogs,
"Go away!"

The dogs went up to Nick.

They looked at the stick.

"Go away," said Nick.

"You are naughty dogs!"
shouted Nick.
"Go inside.
This stick is for my snowman."

Sally said,

"Come here, dogs.

The sticks are not for you.

You can go inside."

"Look, Sally," said Nick.

"Look at my snowman!"